Erotic Distance

Oi, Vlashkin, if you are my friend, what is time?
—Grace Paley, "Goodbye and Good Luck"

WINNER OF THE 2003 T. S. ELIOT PRIZE

The T. S. Eliot Prize for Poetry is an annual award sponsored by Truman State University Press for the best unpublished book-length collection of poetry in English, in honor of T. S. Eliot's considerable intellectual and artistic legacy.

Judge for 2003: C. D. Wright

Erotic Distance

poems by

BARBARA
CAMPBELL

Winner of the 2003 T. S. Eliot Prize

New Odyssey Series
Published by Truman State University Press, Kirksville, Missouri 63501
tsup.truman.edu

Library of Congress Cataloging-in-Publication Data

Campbell, Barbara, 1963—
    Erotic distance : poems / by Barbara Campbell.
        p. cm. — (New odyssey series)
    ISBN 1-931112-31-2 (alk. paper) — ISBN 1-931112-32-0 (pbk. : alk. paper)
    I. Title. II. Series.
    PS3603.A46E76 2003
    811'.6—dc21

                                                    2003007959

Cover art: *Isola*, © Odd Nerdrum, courtesy of Forum Gallery, New York.
Cover design: Teresa Wheeler
Printed by: Thomson-Shore, Dexter, Michigan
Type: Monotype Centaur

∞The paper in this publication meets or exceeds the minimum requirements of
the American National Standard—Permanence of Paper for Printed Library Materi-
als, ANSI Z39.48 (1984).

For Tom

CONTENTS

ACKNOWLEDGMENTS

Grateful acknowledgment is made to the editors of the following journals, in which some of these poems were first published:

Colorado Review: "Mimetic"
Columbia Poetry Review: "The Tyranny of Three"
Denver Quarterly: "Tyranny of Erotic Distance"
Elixir: "The Writing Room," "The Art Lesson," "Chicago Aubade"
Epiphany: "Desire"
Icon: "Painted Vase"
Indiana Review: "Australia"
The Iowa Review: "Quesnay's Aspect"
New American Writing: "Notes on Form," "Foreground," "Parable for a Marriage Long Sought"
No Roses Review: "The Swimming"
Other Voices: "Morning at the Window," "Evening at the Window," "Love Poem in Stricter Measure"
Verse: "Nine Lines Broken into Finer Parts"

Thanks go to The Ragdale Foundation for residencies that afforded the time, space, and privacy necessary for the completion of this book.

My heartfelt gratitude to my parents, Barbara and Glenn Campbell, my brother, Scott Campbell, and my grandmother, Eleanor Campbell, for unending support, love, and humor. Many thanks also to friends and teachers near and far, especially Robert Herschbach, who read each poem with interest and insight, and Paul Hoover, for early and continued encouragement.

And a special thanks to my daughter, Maudie, who is present in every line.

Foreground

A voice speaks, repeating numbers in sequence

encode the ocean within the rock, a statue

wrapped in plastic. The boy

considers two grains—first of sand, then of salt

from which unfolds a City, its language of objects

and *Having begun in your midst*

Encode the statue

wrapped in its own weeping

each number a sequence of flowers in the mouth

fresh air apples all encode unearth

a tenement of miniature trees with light

and running water

Earth clings to the underside of stone

urgent argument for attachment

urgent argument of *Called into being*

my mind is full of you—trenchant frenzied

a zodiac of carved figures a sequence

Encodes the boy with light

a sequence of crude figures cut into the skin

from which unfolds language—the mouth stuffed

with flowers

flagrant, a grain of sand unearths

Animal figure image akin

flagrant, the earth a sea of weeping

from which unfolds

the boy's face sweet apple of light

PARABLE FOR A MARRIAGE LONG SOUGHT

Here is the woman with the visible spine, curled so the woman
of the grave situation, the toiling night
in her place a man burns unconsumed
in her place a room shifts in wild drunken light
the woman who pulled from the horse its spine *eviscerate eviscerate*
who boned the fish, the pheasant and felt no physical pain

Here is the woman whose spine kicks, whose sleep packs
    the languid air
as the room moans the room roars the room
confines the dream his body the chant of days the vegetable
    memory of light

Here is the man with a bone caught crosswise in his throat
who cannot speak his plight
who means no harm
whom the mirror feeds for hours half a day
watch: as the field
watch: as a red house comes in and out of focus for hours
here a man has lost his shoe
here the heart is a fist of linen
watch: as here alights a wasp a sparrow at the high bright windows
there was such speed in my body
transept mirror screen
who cannot speak his plight
watch: as the room confines a dream of bodies arrayed in rows on
    the melting ice

Watch, as here a love poem is composed in strictest light, written
to the packed air to the days arranged sequentially each unsleeping
   here
watch as the dream retells itself:

     once upon a time there was a hundred buttons
     once upon a time the sparrow sought her own descent
     once five months five months I courted
     once let patience have her perfect work:

The economy of light, sighs, secondhand goods, wool & flax,
   animals, birds and ice

THE TYRANNY OF THREE

Each morning my daughter finds
in the bedroom mirror herself. Poem, configure
our life together. Now, the house asleep, the city
asleep under gray rain and the willow's yellow

branches poem include a bearing wall, an aqueduct
and orange poppies pushing through the earth
Poem, ruin Eden, ruin Athens ruin the beautiful
cities, include the music of his face, the advent

of his face preserve Baltimore, where in
Westminster my love lies asleep. Call today faith,
the twenty-fifth beef tallow, call the seventh
lachrymosa, poem, a fig tree reflected

in a copper window. Decry the birth of Simon, all of May
is elemental, decry the birth of Peter the indwelled
fig tree, trunk and fruit indwelled with wasps
"the advent of his face" a crawling knot awash in tallow

In Bill Cass's painting *The Visitation* the four hundred
illuminated figures are missing; the girl who sways
and sings on the car's hood is missing and the kitchen
bathed asleep in light, the thaw we often spoke of

the rain beats missing myself myself myself
S says *in no uncertain terms*; C *feel this*
Poem, quiet the mind hum and pulse my flesh
is punished your flesh wrung of tallow and paint

Poem set quick two seeds in the earth, each morning
my daughter becomes another figure, goes missing, poem
tally the four hundred and weep the birth of Peter

QUESNAY'S ASPECT

Quesnay mimics
in image the orange tree

the seed of which
he carried here from _____, will it grow

O Quesnay
lies in wait, seldom singing

warming the bark in his palms
tonguing the trunk

for fiber and foliate
oath to his vegetable life

In the street we see Quesnay
deep in the thorax of a passerby

deep in the thorax
which carries the heart of a dog

200 years hence and he, a Yankee
at the dog's sweet ear

And the moon
which is fixed or moves

calls the stone street
Bright Snow, calls the tree

Diseases of the Senses
Quesnay, dogged, circles the tree

Brethren shout
against the roar of the carts

sell him to the Ishmaelites
calls the tree Joseph

When he withers the fig tree
salvage one fig

Brethren beckon
the lame dog to the apple tree

already withered
Beckon Quesnay, call Quesnay

the tree which sprang
Ardent busshe that did not waste

CHICAGO GHAZAL

It was enough then to walk beside you, enclosed within the warm
   circle
of your body—my face turned upward in full sun

If I could have, I would have kissed you—my face shadowed by
   your face
on the narrow beach, an everyday crowd, October and the calm,
   finite lake

Instead we walked home—an inscrutable space (By which
   increment
can we measure such loss?) *ziggurat, zamboni,* a backward alphabet a
   paper charm

Now, my daughter draws an ornamental door adorned with ivory,
   cows' teeth
a border of pure lead, square in the exact center of the page

And calls it "the pleasure of his company" "more than my hand
   loves my face"
The sun fixes this vision, now perched—an enormous copper bird

And love, which now reveals itself daily

LANGUAGE

The sheer side of a white house, one
side, a green roof, the sun unrelenting

Inside I am ten. Inside I teach my-
self to count to ten in French. Unrelenting

I have a book. Numbers fall slow, the rope
hanging from a branch or the rope hanging

upstairs, the swing, I was seven and
the sun strikes one side

                         I am seven, maybe
ten, and defined by what comes through the mouth

The swing (a rope), the sun—which has its own
face—and can you see I drink vinegar,

eat weeds eat paper anything eaten
gummed to pulp. It is summer which is one

long day (ten days) one face. I am ten and
in love with my own mouth *huit neuf* which is

a field at night my tongue cuts wheat in the dream

LAMENT FOR A SON

The children come home shouldering good light
home, its walls of woven grasses, yellow glass the landscape
the color of blood flesh excrement

the landscape shudders—their heads incline their heads tilt up
my boy a bright fish a knot of vein
in my palm the darkest river in history

now in reply to the body: strict wrist
muffled tongue the landscape shudders—the children
come home in a clutch eyes hollow mouths open

tongues of jumping fish, the boy a knot of light

my body leans out the yellow window
now in reply to the landscape: now color swarms
a river of yellow grasses

the children tilt in strict light
the children come home a wall of flesh
a glass jar swarms with fish; the river swarms with blood

now in reply my boy sets the jar on the riverbank empty
the body the mercy of such an inversion
my boy comes home hollow body woven tongue

the dark river tilts jumps—my body a wall of light inclined

Morning at the Window

In my absence my daughter learns
to knot a length of yellow cord
clumsy at the front window she sits
intent over her work and whispers
the story of her birth: *at 4:16 pm the clouds cracked open*, and so on

In her absence I sit eating a soft-cooked egg
my fingers slick with yolk
one hundred pink geraniums bloom
white in their pots

In my absence she learns to live in two worlds at once
carrying my image in her head, my image growing
dim as she draws face after face—dour mouths
across a clean page

She sleeps on a secondhand mattress, sterilized
under a blanket of white eyelet, red worsted
at the height of day
dreaming vase after vase of red tulips
tangerine gladiolus taller than she

She wakes and two vases remain, each empty
each standing as I left them in her window

Tyranny of Errant Desire

Out of my window I whisper *love*
to my neighbor who coughs
over freshly cut wood, seared meat

and purple lilies. Poem, take a lover—
Because I am one of the faithful
there lies a torso in Darby Creek, a body

at the bottom of a lake. Out of my window
I whisper *garments, timber, shrimp* and a world
away, a lily blooms, milk-white for export. *Love* I say

and my daughter falls, milk-white to sleep
As the bird falls under the car's wheel
its soul—released or consumed—*sirrah*

becomes a whole number—*Love* I say
and its body lies, unburned
and burning, tongue split *take heed* and whispers

Take heed, sirrah, the whip Love and
thus does meter bloom from its bitten tongue

Poem, these penciled figures; we sense
the body, the lip of a deep lake
an act of theft, the body lifting

Poem, mine this rich vein *Bloom* I say
and the young man in gallery 236 lays dying
his eyes *aggressive palliative* race

over the kneeling River God—
the muscled trunk an inverse lily
Herein lies the bird's call, its burnt tongue *love*

his eyes faithful—O private, unpardoned
sin—Poem three figures support a man
(and a smaller sketch of the same)

In gallery 236 a man, *sirrah*, lies burning
Sparrows lift the body aggressed upon
Poem, I have an hour

Notes on Form

Six branches fix the sky, these near
leafless, black, perpetually wet
Those—sketchy, a dizzy knit of one-
in-three over blue shed and yard; a figure

is missing. The sky thickens
the paint, coarse flesh

to be rendered, clear light to fix
house alley house pinned back, pinned
down, everything scraped, as it was, into place
Describing itself, meticulous, branch *ad*

infinitum branch, house—the ground
laid open the whole sweep physical still
only the colors coming up—the slate
roof a sheety lake, a whole field

lights up. Now the figure
is distant, the figure is still

missing, stilting the picture, deep
in lyric a metric
of days we keep what keeps us

He will lead us through a situation. Having
rendered him in clear light, I can see him

clearly, making his way to the lake
He is a loose shingle, he unhinges

myth. We are led
to the roof, the lake,

the jewel as in *this lake, a ~ nestling amid mountains*
So close, his left foot, left leg, his whole
right side, the water fit with jewels and dark
brown up to his neck up to the struts

of the bridge, the lake giving into a river
a wild tilt, no longer stone
or glass, just the rush-mesh-spill and two
loose goats nosing the mud he sees

three loose goats, a trio
watching from the bank as *in amid the mountains, One face*

Now he scrapes the bridge,
scrapes white paint from the still
bridge struts. We are led

We cannot see the brow straight coarse or fine
We cannot see the wide thin mouth,

the jewel of his hand the jewel
of his face rendered

in thickening paint

TYRANNY OF EROTIC DISTANCE

As we pass the common garden, the body
eats cake in bed. As we pass the agony
in the garden—he swims within my body
him what rocks the knife

The garden blooms and fruits, cardinal
to the arteries of the earth—poem become
a dowry of fruits, revocable dowry
relieve this body, this garden of salts.

Poem, I dreamt four nights ago
at midnight I broke into song, I dreamt into song
this body; this orchard rains down
salts like fruit, salt unto fruits

and *Enter Brutus into his orchard*

The knife spins in the river, swollen
at dawn, its errant blade an apogee
its errant blade this body
swollen at dawn, the garden waits

A man and a woman wait—*Enter Brutus*

The knife sings in the river, whispers
(*O him what whispers*) in the river's ear;
their feet unshod and shifting in the river's bed
limbs akimbo with the current—a cardinal

bright bit of flotsam—singing still

Snags in a mouth of rock, snags rock
my body lies at midnight, full
of song exhausted—mouth full of salt
exalted *him what rains and fruits*

REPLICATE

A man wakes, enraged. Where is his eye his hand his leg? Instead
he sees a dish of wood, a water rat, a wax figure. On Christmas Day
1938 my grandparents took in Ira, a lame boy with a weak heart.
His mother, furious, sick drove through New York empty and
desperate; a man pushed stones into a field, building a wall. By
spring the field floods the wall stands and the man wakes, enraged.
He falls through the field—falls through landscape to another
landscape, another flooded field. With a pebble he sketches into
the rock's sheer face his hand, his eye, his own face. Ira died four
months later, drowned in a man-made lake. He stands beside my
grandfather, who later painted him, a winged figure a replica in a
decorative fresco of griffins and dolphins. The man wakes to the
form and image of his own face. Burning with grief a woman paces
the orchard. Two thousand years before Christ, the Minoans built
the palace at Knossos with its walled pit, orchard and gypsum
quarry—a labyrinth of painted light. Into a large public bath of
stone the water is still running. Into the empty cistern a dim figure
dumps bowl after broken bowl. The man wakes on the threshing
floor and painted there in fresco, two thousand figures enraged,
hand leg and furious eye all within reach, each image intact—a
branch still burning—his own face and there I confine him,
turning his blind ear to the wind.

PAINTED VASE

This is not a modern story.
This is a Russian elegy with a red vase, an alphabet
I trace
the letters, their declension and later
from some distance they shout back
pallid and *tumult* and rest
finally on a small desk under an unfinished painting
and small red vase.

Here is the story:
There are rows of painted trees, rows swaining
the low slope of hill. The moon hangs for two days
at 10 a.m. visible, thrilling the flat
blue field of sky a whole quarter
tube of blue, cadet, cerulean;
sky blued up
around the flat gray apple flesh

Of a boy, but he's not there. No
one is painted in yet, compelled by simple red apples
or a red squirrel bred
for the clamor and limit of trees
and the next minute

and the next minute is the painter's trace, a line
to guide the boy, lover or herdsman, to the vase
painted in the right quarter
of the canvas, level with
the limit of trees.

This will be his first world:
The red vase and fluid body
of the squirrel, bloated, fluid then bloated again.
He will stare at color soaked
in light, trace his finger up the tree
bark and shout the name he sees there

the shame of my

love O love I will never leave here

as light

falls on the broken neck, on every articulated
bone. A red vase of buffed glass—
handled passed & set the body pressed
flat, a dun hand,
palm and flesh quick-stroked
The tricks of light on tree bark the apples The vase
sits, a smear of color
a closed bowl of pooled blood
base & neck

crooked, unsexed, a brown slur of water mixing
with sinew, reared for this my love the limit and clamor of trees

MISREAD

In mid-October, my daughter reads *summer* as *sycamore*
She knows the rules for silence, when to speak one's name

At six, she reads *champion* as *chimpanzee*—at six
Has known unbearable love, unbearable sadness
                                        And I have too

She spells *rth, silck* the sycamore, vainglorious bursts
Open into orange one morning—and ten words by sight

The sun enters the underworld / any coin buys 12 minutes

An ancient coffin of imported sycamore carries a girl
Who, motherless, cannot be protected and cannot be helped
                                        The sun enters the underworld

Up from the ground, now neither hurt nor slowed
An ancient coffin of sycamore, imported to this river bed

My dear, I press into your hand this book
which reads as follows:

The way grief unearths us—how at thirteen
That girl was pleased with thousands of rams, ten thousand
        rivers of oils
                                        And I was too

In February, my daughter dreams a boy fishing
in spring mud and in fishing brings up a mitten

That boy, my daughter's friend, turns his sweet face
And measured thus in syllabics: *the river was a constant hazard*

The sycamore sways in the late sun—
Every minute we have another minute gone

The monkeys make sorrowful noise overhead

MIDDLE GROUND

Most days I worked without stopping
a painted figure girded to the wall, a swirl of metal the swung
      wheel
a winged figure watched in the branches bright burden of visible
      song

Dear Schellmann the ocean glitters as gold upheaves the heads of marigolds
      adrift in a river

Most days I worked without stopping
unburdened of song from my hand unfolds a vine
fruited blossomed begotten

From my hand a bright eye watched in the branches, avid
In the darkest part of the house there is a painting, a gabled house
its flowers open at the height of day—most days

I watch the light change, the ocean a middle ground a marigold
      placed in the hand

Most days in my ardor I place a mirror in the open window
      my face adrift
in full sun—a trapped bird circles in the topmost room
and drops, avid river of unburdened light

Five Odes for Ellen Gunderson

after Michael Palmer

Laying aside his earthly form, black mud and stabbing grasses
an atmosphere resplendent
with middle division—sky and ground sky and ground—mouth
    open

Leaving behind the pitch and heft of the roof—prospect of face,
    prospect of arms
Ellen we are never here where we are

Three bare trees sing wait, are later soaked in gasoline, set ablaze—
    mouth shut

The choked cries of a chained hound—the cant of each ear
turned toward and away from the west-facing window my face,
    Ellen
and three white doors—of *Water* of *Cloth* of *Air and Light*

The sky opens—uncertain image—a stone burns in his arms
and lights his face resplendent

With nothing between as in vision, azure and flecks the
    windowpanes that same blue

Division, Ellen, desperate regret of decisions, my ear pressed
    to the reaching tree
which may contain a verbal illustration
see *Atmosphere* see *Audible Sobs*

A vertical column
of mercury—under standard gravity, the dog sleeps

in a closed room, the sky pales pink and the sun Ellen, arcing into
    the trees

THE WRITING ROOM

Now outside my window a red tree deepens toward black
I looked to see where we could cross the water
Which aches with beauty, historical fact

Notwithstanding, surely vexed, a woman steps—looks back
Unquiet her eye and footbridge dumb witness to slaughter
Now outside my window a red tree deepens toward black

As creeds prayers and songs unlearnt—as water pours over her
    back
I watched the little body unbend, grow straight, my daughter
Will ache for beauty, historical fact

As four lashed saplings, as a day of tasks
In relic, knuckle, coin and bone I sought I sought
Outside my window the red tree growing black

Past the dooryard, into the earth—a river of blood, intact
Pours over lintel, doorpost, stunted tree sweet fodder
For beauty, not fact

The woman wakes to perfect flight; the river of blood goes black
Unlearnt, unsung beside her turning—Across the water
outside my window a red tree deepens, turns back
And aches with beauty, historical fact

AUSTRALIA

It is September first and the first day
of spring. A girl, thinking, stands at the edge
of an open field. She does not see pattern or
advantage, only someone
at home. Someone's there,
an elbow testing the temperature

of a lemon-scented bath, or sitting
unopposed in the trees outside thinking,
Sing. Someone is singing. It is September first,
first breath and ladder under
us to summer and
the girl stands in a stand of walnut trees

thinking I ran here with my neck broken
(fir tree, evergreen) with my head held in
my hands. I will whittle a small ladder, a fire
the mercy of September
seven lemon trees
for every yard. In an open field

in Australia a girl stands alone
in a duffel coat. She has six stripped sticks
six broken elbows broken open in her coat
She ran here, her neck intact
hating her white neck
and I am there with her, handing her sticks

six, seven—all cut with a small steel knife.
She and I will never dance arm-in-arm
together, as if we never felt the passed bone
handle of the knife, as if
this wasn't a field
of onions, as if we found a meadow

in a mud field of onions and under
us, the trees. We will never dance, only
push the bulbs of spring onions, each an aureole
over the knife blade, missing
the bone and singing
what we pass and hold; what mercy between us.

Nine Lines Broken into Finer Parts

All the day and until evening the steady invective of armature

which felled me thus about my neck; a boy hones his throwing knife

And hits soft mortar—the auricle of each ear pressed to the cellar
wall

Here we learn that money is money and rope is rope and merely
fractive

Who lived on locusts and wild honey, attar, phalanx and
fingerbone

The forgotten humors of the body—and stone which becomes
ritually unclean

Five years the house was silent deep in its work and asleep in her
room

All around her such sweetness sweetness the shadow of flight
across my skin

Scissors the width and wingspan of passing birds—paint cut fine
by this knife

TO THE TREES' IRREGULAR TREMOR

My horse crops
Knee-deep in the flooded garden
Knee-deep in the flooded garden
My love mucks out the garden shed
His face a haze of smoke
Ten more miles, it is Wisconsin
Where he sits, fixed
Wishing the mint and coltsfoot would grow
Forever fixing a broken spigot
Just as well
I am at the mercy of my body

The near trees shiver
All night they drip and tick and just through them
Weeds flower in the open field
All night my love spins a wing nut
Over and over a rusted bolt
And one hornet begins his nest

I try to still myself and can't
While roses bloom
on the rusted chaise behind me
She lifts a cold glass of gin
He strikes a match
To the trees' irregular tremor
Under which the horse, croup hip haunch and fetlock, sleeps
In a gesture of great hope
A crow flies west

Now the hornet strains at one's brain
dear James you are dead
And I am at the mercy of my body
Everything exhales
Just as well
I have come a long way, to surrender my body
To the body of the horse

Tyranny of the Aerial Map

The gods of the earth turn, lie prone and weep
the gods of the earth turn and a man
emerges, red from the yellow ground

And I feel tenderly / a tenderness
toward him turns the English-speaking world
poem, cripple leg mind hand and heart—assume

Tenderness; seat him at the curbside, weeping
or race the man into the rain, alone
poem, *I am a blasted tree* turn

Fowl, beef, linen and of every good—numbers
poem, yearn for the figure, for the figure
which swims up *for abuse or nurture*

My daughter turns in her sleep—a tenderness
emergent in the earth—and the earth weeps
and ticks its shrinking heart; the gutters flood

No good will come of numbers, poem, the waking
dream of night; row upon row of figures
swim up swim up and lie strewn, livid there

Upon the grass. A yellow ground supplants us,
daughter, weep and weep each livid figure turns
poem, learn this: the yellow trees at evening

PRIVACY

Our story takes place
with a prize deer in a square yard
curled against a cyclone fence
It lives its life here—
feeds from the stream the yellow grass
The conceit of the deer
leg crosses leg—its bones
the light still, direct
refracted from the fence posts
And now
the paltry untreed yard—a garden
the fence—a stone wall—
all too sudden the celandine
nasturtium the yellow flood
of light and trees
lean or bursting from grief
O gentle doe
unfolded *sweet jesus*
from that mossy wall
we are with you, our story begins
here, behind this vaulted wall
you see
Our city is a wreck already, flee
with horse and cart
flee on your donkey
wreathed in red
carnations, yellow roses
the deer flees
And we are alone

Lyric on a Painting by Odd Nerdrum

Here, hung above the world
Two figures hover—the meat of air
legs rigid, the sky in silent rant
of disuse injury disease
the right eye viscid, indirective
I slept and did not dream

If the body's fixed—one aspect
of rapture—the mouth moves in song
O pool of fixéd light—my beloved
a wealth of rendered objects
pear bread and brick, two figures
unseat a third, encircle his body, a built world

His body twinned in shankbones,
the sound of the mare
in her suffering—I did not dream

I did not dream, atrophy in strophes
apes song the head
bent at the neck, face to the pool—terminus
of delicate chemistry awry
Esophagus swelled, tongue swelled a pearl
in the throat—terminus of light

Of light the fourth figure's made
and stills the viscid air
A fifth figure with grief as her aspect
five fingers cover her mouth

five fingers cover her eyes
Intermittent echolalia

You can find me here
without boy or bird
singing the burnt world its rapture

BLURB

Here are lyrics of heartbreaking directness and candor:

First the marrow grows thick, the bones heat up
one hundred forty-eight whale bones of varying width and held
on my tongue a soaked cake of sugar

My neighbor pees, fucks, smokes all night; a man
shoots from his window three times a gun
And springs there in my heart a tree

and into even more ambitious territory

Beloved, my love, a mirror swung too fast at the face and not to be
    outdone
not to be undone, I swung back

in whose palpable solitude

One hundred forty-eight bones, which
One hundred forty-eight bones, stitched as a fence, which
for the whale, approximate teeth—the heat rises
the bones heat up; a cake of sugar soaked in kerosene feeds this
    small blue flame

Retreated into pathless country

Beloved my love reduced in body—two hundred six bones
and with one correct cut we fall in, the body drops

What if a woman stood waiting
what if this garment stitched of bones this conception, second
    cage of ribs
illustrates the swell and containment my heart
is nothing more than strict pleasure, calumny, queer dream

the elusive and intimate anthropology of water

the poet wrote «it seemed a kind of heaven there» but what does
    he know? Him, with his acre of hissing grass, his oaks folding
    into lake light. He was small and clean and fine, I think. His
    heart one hundred utterances of beauty, his heart

Beloved, my love, where can I locate this? Arm, lung, spine and
    heart
all carefully affixed in tin—doscientos milagros

sense of one's body, a stable hierarchy of values

What if the tree drops a single yellow leaf—resettles around this
    small loss?

of that buried past

shitty shitty shitty
In Ezekiel's valley of bones

dissociative reflections

In the topmost room of the house, the wind
whipped all around me and bone knit with bone

the waste of pain

in the topmost room of the house (I wrote this once) the bird
  circles once and sings its life—but what did I know? That bird
  flew and flew until it dropped
from flesh to sinew to dry bone—it just flew, stupid, until it died
and came to rest on my desk, beshitted such as it was

in the end, humanness shows forth nobly

please forgive me—if I don't write this down, I'll forget:
what if a child is born from his own absence
turned from the cracked rib, the forced sway

over and over, without end

I will come out to meet you as far as I will come

In the topmost room of the house—we wished
to sleep there, but no one could lift the bed
to the window

LOVE POEM IN STRICTER MEASURE

to GSC

The sun in this story is not just a physical fact

I rode a horse along a narrow ridge
as each tree fell blazing into the lake

each tree a reprieve
a door into the earth, each tree

Unutterable landscape
a lake of yellow gingko leaves

the sun in this story is not just a physical fact
the sun in this story, a stocked lake of blind fish

deep lake in the earth this story I rode a horse
blazing into the lake

And on the earth his body lies, face down
the cold pool trembles; the trees align and bend

Lying on the earth a lake of silent weeping

AGAINST ANIMISM

On the last warm night I looked
into the beak of the finch
and saw my own crooked mouth

I looked into the belly
of the lion and Robert~
my mouth filled with honey

On the last warm night *Nicanor*
lie dead in his harness, eyes
fixed on the coffered ceiling

mouth filled with honey, his mind
a riot of locusts, jaw-
bone in flux, his legs a-twitch

on the threshing room floor
O separable life, century
hedged, a burnt marsh—the story gone

On the last warm night Nicanor
awash in dull sun, the seeds
of life awake in his spine

amphibians fishes wink
and cry O century O
grid for the cities a grid

for each dead city lies etched
in their heads. On the last warm
night I looked into the eye

of the finch and saw a boy
alone on a frozen beach
(the wrists of Nicanor erupt

in sympathy) the fish in
his fists *moving accidents*
of flood and field cry

for the silent vast Pacific
he runs, from one end one drop
of honey on his tongue

O century O hedge O seed
of the cities, winks the dull sun

THE ART LESSON

Of these four brick houses pick one:
draw the roof's sudden pitch
the cupola, turret, and finally the tree line—white with ice

the poem begins: a body much diminished
the room dismantled roundly brick by brick
the bed stripped, the room askew

my love eats a sweet bruised apple
my love in rhythmic circular precision
squats on his haunches, my love which indicates movement,
    a proving ground

Deep in the pitted brick another voice shouts up out of me:

When I went up the apple tree
all the apples fell on me

I admonish: of these four rooms you must choose
inside a girl makes good the destruction of a bird
plate by plate in stark gravure
each image rolled from her shoulder
each image a body much diminished

Another voice shouts up out of me:

I admonish: make honey in your mouth pull aside your skirt
Her heart a silverfish, her belly a tide pool my love
eat this poem my love

A moving illustration with one distant swimmer
who cannot speak for her rhythmic circular precision

Now, reach into the quiet for the name of the beloved
Into the mouth of the apple
the brain of the fish lost to us now
in the belly of the wrecked bird
in the still belly of the cold pool

Evening at the Window

Snow falls from a white sky—I send my body out walking and
     watch it go
through a break in the fence following a white path in the buried
     grass

It does not turn or wave; birds sit just below the grassline insistent,
     stoic, focused
in the buried grass a torn rabbit, ravaged by fox or crow, I wrap my
     hands

at my ribs which ache and ache sometimes, breathing *now my body,*
     not my own
a figure of membrane, phosphorous, vascular light

A body of light walks unadorned, shorn of hair a harp of bones
     this ribcage
ladder of bones broken, laid bare *my own* a cage of air and
     breathlines

My hand carries the rabbit's carcass my body my body comes back
I locate myself in no natural occurrence *now my body, not my own*

volcano tidal storm tumult earth's orange fissures no weather
     pattern no stars
or their meshwork over the earth, the blood of an animal, sap
     of a plant

I send my body away from my body *not my own*

ABANDONED PARADELLE

Consider this line your painted eye, a paper charm
Consider this line your painted eye, a paper charm
Which acts as a devotion; it blooms daily in my palm
Which acts as a devotion; it blooms daily in my palm
Consider this my devotion which blooms, painted in your eye
A daily charm, a palm line; it acts as paper

In a story about enclosure, hunger and shorn hair
In a story about enclosure, hunger and shorn hair
The man circles six times the garden, a girl his ziggurat
The man circles six times the garden, a girl his ziggurat
In hunger, the shorn garden circles a girl—a story about
time's enclosure, the man, six ziggurats, hair

And any animal awaiting slaughter—his arm encased in ice
And any animal awaiting slaughter—his arm encased in ice
Outside the window six painted scenes and you, stiff with grief
Outside the window six painted scenes and you, stiff with grief
And the slaughter you painted in ice, encased outside the window
Awaiting any arms and the animal grief—with six stiff scenes

Consider this line my ziggurat, my painted garden, my window
The shorn girl painted the man—circles his daily slaughter
Consider my hair, it blooms in ice, a stiff animal six times my
    devotion
Outside, a garden of paper scenes: grief, hunger, enclosure
Consider this line—eye arm palm which acts as a story
Awaiting you, within my palm a paper charm encased

LINES RECLAIMED FROM FAITH

The plane flies west, a steady stream of smoke
or light from the wings, artifice
of longing, trickery of what is missed

Descending print in a book to my right
and who holds a pill under
his tongue, intent on the argument—drag and lift

                                                  for flight

Because I am deaf in my right ear *where
is her daughter* I cannot hear
the yowls of a cat—caged and stowed—*failure*

to thrive; the plane is dark. As we descend
my body, my fingers swell
During the morning, nine basil seeds cracked

Open and pushed roots in, stems up—*Husband,
the plane is dark.* Having left
the city, its division religious

Façade of rocks, hidden frieze of red rocks
during the morning, rhetoric
of ascent, a riot of windows—pink going

to red—"The Cavalry at Gettysburg"
a working sheep farm the church
plain brick, built round windows built to peak

and hold each voice *let's call home* my body
like a physic—plain brick
the swelled ague of voice—the plane is dark

The book recants its logic—block by block—
from the first high point, nine seeds,
until one word remains—offal of down-

turning revision. In the cellar one
head in fine white stone, shrouded
the Kaiser in effigy on a stretcher

If the dark plane falls, I will be a woman
poised in tintype, wholly deaf
my hip and elbow canted left, fallen

at the bottom of a curved staircase, leaves
will flourish in my teeth, my breast
for the birds that see him, for their feasts' delight

fourteen hours, sixteen hours
at some point in time
the city will collapse from (a) Construction,

or (b) This Equation: *'twixt*
the muck and the golden crown
"they often trap red fox in this field"

When the city falls *a Christening* our legs
will thin and buckle under
shimmy hazy pace our weight—we will press

our fingers into the rock's palm
and call it Faith, in florid bloom
plants will sway over us—we will heave

Rock into paving stone and call it a road

CHICAGO AUBADE

This is the image I meant for you: myself
painting a sere orchard
painting the decorative border oblique allusion
myself
immersed in the oils' aroma
I begin with the border: burnt orange
with a horde of monkeys, rabbits, seed pearls
the curved fronds of the common fern
each an echo—the way my body bent to meet your body
and bent back as we slept under a bowed window
I rose first then you rose—a tree in which hung
ten hornets' nests thrummed in your dream,
bent almost to the earth but stood
as you removed no nest and only echoed tenfold

In that moment, I turned my face to this page
to imagine the days ahead
to build a picture (for which I will be forgiven)
a flat expanse with one or two moving parts
a flat aspect
This is the image I meant for you
in the center of that orchard—the dream of spring—hornets
gnaw bare the green twigs, and branches bend
to their descent
to the faint aroma of stunted fruit
I woke first, while the orchard sleeps, with a necklace
of rapeseed, beads turned from the bovine horn

a necklace
of horsehair, the room hung with rabbit skins
I woke first and turned my face to your face
a flat aspect—the dream of spring—I woke first then you woke
This is the image I meant for you

TYRANNY OF ADVENT

In a clearing, one hundred birds take flight
of the body—the upward gust of time—
O dispassionate act, my daughter wakes

up seven years old *him what pity wakes*
in the crotch of a tree, learns "severally,
as the perfect wife and husband," to work

by hand the gussets, gather, asseverate
Poem beneath us lie hills of pure salt
the gathering house—the tree becomes

a tin horn, a garment of salt, a tree
ablaze—one hundred incarnadine fruits

In a clearing, a hill of red ants seize
the body; poem pull the quick from the meat
pity the body its gussets, pity

the service tree, pity the anguished
hundreds, poem O *several fruits so given*
What wakes in the tree is perfect flight

memory dictates a dull sun, a sap
green hue, a quick hedge speaks
from a crotch of earth, thrown open

the body sheds its salts and rests, ablaze

THE BUILDER'S WIFE

to RH

We stand—two bodies of action
two bodies of fact
all action in the language, the blank
of days, the days erased

Like a man who built a house in a dream
and wakes exhausted to say *we stand*

And a solid white bird, sights trained
on the vertical, lights above
the coupled door—half-built half-had
the hasps attached to the white spruce planks

The wood's stasis astonishes us and
the man, still building
builds his house around the bird,
preserves an eave and its own clean nest
and at night, asleep in the ease
of the other's breathing, he dreams
a mountain of flowers, a hill of white trees

They love and a field burns, circled by dogs—

Are they bees or the blooms
of flowers—one thousand particular flowers—
or the brown bodies of wasps?

We are one body, left in the open to rot
to the violence of dogs
our spine, like time, is pressed to the earth
our flank burns and burns our lustral bones
and streams the land with fat

We are one bird and its own geography—in verticals and ecstasy

We are one day, open to the even lines of time

MIMETIC

with a fragment from Berryman

The horse grew mad with hunger
and air your body's made, and moves—a verse
inviolate intractable animal devours spring
in a lonely house from whose body issues an emblem

and air your body's made, and moves—a verse
circles once and sings its life—shut up without water
in a lonely house from whose body issues an Emblem
of Glorious Day an Emblem of Brack and Pulp

circles once and sings its life—shut up without water
grown old with longing from standing water she cries in verses
of the glorious day an emblem of brack and pulp
mimetic a hybrid an apple her body devours itself

grown old from longing she cries in verses from water
issues a glorious hunger—her body moves
mimetic a hybrid an apple her body devours itself
The horse grew mad with hunger

LINES DISCARDED AND DEEPLY FELT

Into the bark of an alder tree, I carved my name

and woke

years later dreaming of you

of donkeys being driven over grain

Sunday morning at the JCC swimming pool I come to the latter of
    two limiting points

in time

the boy leaps into the carrying stream

is wingless

a hedge opens, their heaven below the earth

a dish of wood, a little grave, a wax figure

and heaven's envy of the open earth

is wingless and runs about alone over the soil by day

days it happens

through the floor one man drowns

of donkeys being driven over grain

birds coupled mid-flight

each Friday my body opens to close on Sunday

the body falls and falls and falls and finally lies

a dish of wax, a little wood, a grave figure

my body opens

the boy leaps into the carrying stream

unearthed

uncarried

the mouth stuffed with leaves, shoved full of dirt, stuffed with
    flowers

at the root of my tongue

birds coupled mid-flight

to my left a tree of eyes to my right

the figure of a man floats faintly above the girl

the day of rest forthcoming

I dreamt of cities, expanses of water of affect of bloodstream

where have you gone, beloved boy

now that all the birds of the earth hover at my hands

is wingless

days it happens

days it happens

days it happens

THE SWIMMING

A woman is nothing but water swelling she is swimming
she is driving a nail, standing ankle deep in
the sand with her mother.

If there are four fish there is one fish one
whale swimming in her just this: a metaphor
for fish—her, inside it.

The vaginal space is a kind of metaphor and not a
fish, an animal or bottle. The obvious
connotes it: more swimming.

The words *vaginal* and *space* create
distance—these words are difficult; they lay down and
sleep. They are words waiting.

To walk away is difficult; there is no likening
to that. Nothing stops, but lays, waits, always
swelling. Leaving becomes a lack of immediate action.

A woman is nothing. Ornament is not natural,
fountain or half-covered book. There are poles
and chemicals, endless her breathline.

Nothing and a gate; vaginal. And space
sits around it. A woman is contained in
that space. Delphinium.

Delphi and *delphinium* come from one continuum.
Internal like swimming. Nothing but her breaths which come
pitched to her at distance.

Repetition falls hand over hand. One
plant four fish all absent, blank. Blue is also
absent. Blue is pinking.

The words vaginal and space repeat in pattern
like a breathline. However oracular one
woman, she is nothing and not a gate. A space will contain her.

EPITHALAMION: HOW WE DROWN

1. beach

Now that we know this and name it,
this first rough plunge, this sudden
singing in the blood—the stupid beauty of two
heads—intact on the rocks

Now I will bear your head
on my hips at the water's edge, poke
in the rocks for lost teeth, shorn
hair and find my voice where I found
it—in your mouth. And my heart,
the clam and radish, my tears
set out in seven little dishes
all that is bitter, clenched, all poured out
and found here.

The wet black asking beach alive now
with rocks and psyche and see them—sunk
and died in the sea's hidden
ear. A curve of rocks—the ocean's
trees—green, tongued, one hundred
tongues, one hundred ears.

2. body

And who splits who parts this beauty, the dark
flesh of white fish which
sound the depth deeper and hear

us—sounding from the ocean's cold middle
to sink and rise and live. This life

Begins. In pots of hot salted water,
in salmon and in the eggs of salmon
issued into the mouth
of water, a river's running bed
an ocean opening into itself. We are that
ocean and swimming in it, breathing easily
Out of the lung's stomach and into
the blood—iron muscle and asphalt song,
humming over and under
our skins, salt and basalt in desperate song.
Held furious and separate—two skins
that cool and peel and cool again, colder at depth. Don't

Leave me to this—to the struck feet, struck
and sunk from the sun's imperative
To the shriveled nipples fisted
tight in a cold soaked breast, to the small fish
left swimming in the tight dish of hips,
dumb with love. Sink slowly.
Sink in rhythm, sink only as I
sink, in my skin, singing unvoiced
by love. We

3. *song*

Can live here.
On the cold floor, never waiting never
baited, stinking of bait. Our lips
thicken, our mouths become bladders of song and fish

Swim away from us. We are deep, past
mouth and bed, in constant black,
our clock and mythic singing. We have
lyric, a rough metric of days
dark as night, in which we still dream
a thin blue canal running along
the ocean, now locked solid in iron
and salt. We dream a light open boat,
red and rocked from foot to foot,
dry bodies, wet
fingers light on the water's light. We wake

To the sight of trees, the sound of breathing
the air's rush in the ear our brilliant
hair, pulling us up
to the beach, body and song. We wake
to the other's eyes, the brightest thing we see.

TYRANNY OF THE PRESENT MOMENT

In the absence of birds singing
the beak and ears of a hare
the deer bellowing—poem

pity this assignation in the garden
pity the bellowing—fluent in fat
sulfur honey blood and bones

In the absence of his body
I recommend to the Earth
sugar wheat rice and soap

To my right, the bare tree sings—
the hare nailed up—herewith
I recommend the tree

in strict congress
with his body I sing   *Dear Schellmann*
                          they are perishing Jews

And pours forth from the Earth
a garden of bones—herewith
red lilies bloom in a slanting rain

the bare tree sings
sin enters
at the eyes the heart, poem

wash the body sing
this indignity

Dear Schellmann
I am perished save my ear

LINES APPROXIMATING LIGHT

I am drawn my love to the ruined
    arena, drawn by the wind and strewn brick
        and dreaming I pull body after body from the pit

The red earth rich in lead, the blankness utters
    my name ever outward—all the dying grasses
        my love *her eye is closed shut* call up the image

Of a house closed shut, now standing now ruined
    the strewn earth—a quiet sobbing from the next room
        fourteen thousand blinded men pulling bodies

Up from the mud; fourteen thousand blinded men
    all draw the same house, call up the image
        of bleeding grasses the blankness closed shut

CHICAGO PASTORAL

Above my head, woven and fringed
on a blue ground of irregular variegate
O Body my dumb love
five goats crouch at the water to drink
the pond, a lazy oval, is stitched as such
the goats' heads bend there in pairs
and one— the male I think—larger, darker
with four red hooves
rears up with joy at his dominion
all around him indigenous plants
bend toward and away from the water
they circle, their growth horizontal, wingish, which bears out
as above they become figures or angels, grow heads
in red concentric rings, one is white and even
O Body an opened book
the next is grandest—Plantagenet—
the third a tree of cherries or dwarf apples but still
we must return to the brindle goat, his red hooves, his beauty
outshines even Pan, for once covered,
who stands at the water's edge, in profile
his eye wild, lips red at his pipe
elsewhere, a Tang Dynasty horse
crops the grass at the base of a tree
he is tied there, and happily so—eyes down, he crops
he crops in the dawn's gray calm
and opposite, in a lithograph (I cannot see)
which reflects my east window, its arching tree of cherry or
        dwarf apple
And under which pushes up a row of orange lilies year after year

Flies an angel, his hand at the muscled flank
of a lion, and something like a winged horse
Behind them, a storm gathers in ominous crosshatch
O Body in truth only kin to birdflight, become visible just
    a moment
Sprig of broom, a passing note
Five cut lilies drop their petals one by one
and outside my window a goldfinch waits
to marvel at the beauty of the human body
for my subject
for it all to go to seed—late nester
a godsend at this the height of summer

DESIRE

Every organ is a song. The black lungs
Sung or singing, a song sung
Running up a road, in Greek, singing
Every freckled left arm left
Lying along the table's edge,

The legs bowed open or straight
And the face *O God the face* a chorus

Of song. Every live thing in
The house is stilled. I do
Not want your hands but I
Want them on me, still, in the middle
Of that road, singing, desire singing—always

The soft idiot—softly, *me*. To dream
Of you—of the solid

Body, solid and not, in a ring
Of girls, your whole world a skirt
And arms raised up and rising
All around you
The living thing, the song I know
Finally through

The mouth and vowel, chorus and house
Finally, softly, *me*

GENESEO

Among the Finns, immigrant children in a one-room schoolhouse,
    you are posed.

Sitting closest to you—in the picture I have—a girl with a head
larger than any man's. I imagine you showed her great kindness and
no pity. I imagine you also in the rooming house with other
women—all teachers, each rising early in her own neat room.

Each morning my daughter tells this story:

His dog ran away; the boy grew tired
His sister hides in a flame-red hedge

Each day she begins again—a new page in her sure hand.

In that schoolhouse there was a stove, your desk, a wall of north-
facing windows where the sun moved in its broad arc as the
children learned our difficult alphabet, the run of numbers. The
lunch pails steamed neatly beneath the row of coats.

But I know nothing more of those children, nothing of the work
their parents came to do. At each geography lesson you carefully
included Finland, traced on the map its outline, but they grew
older, married and that image paled under our constant sun.

And then they only dreamt it—the birch twigs, copper, zinc and
silver—the surface of sixty thousand lakes.

Today the rain comes straight down.

Today I tell you this; I dreamt it: Three men travel a great distance
and rest at the edge of a stilled lake. They sleep, pray and make
their soup of beef, radish, spinach and egg. I know nothing of their
lives, or the dark geography of their desires. The rain comes
straight down. I trace their faint path from a great distance.

My daughter sits beside me. Today I will leave her at the
schoolroom door—clean, warm and brightly lit. The white sun
rises as if from a great lake.

She turns her page and writes:

The boy ran away; his dog grew tired
One girl hides in a place
so small I cannot find her

Tyranny

In the center of your palm a pill becomes a nickel
becomes a sparrow which takes flight—your full name rolls
from its tongue, love in dumb show—the body lies

The bird dives lights teaches a dog to sing
Husband, tongue your maps—breathe—the body lies
Wife, become the broadest sense of loss with ear pressed to palm

An ear pressed to the middle of the brilliant day

INVECTIVE

Bodies becoming other bodies, breathe—my boy is sick
whose head swings blind by day, whose blood lymph saliva
was but recently enclosed within a tree—limbs stript
fruits stript and littered the ground with butchered beasts

Whose heads swing blind by day whose blood lymph saliva
run from his knife, run from my boy over the soil and pierce his
    thigh
his fruits stript; the ground littered with butchered beasts
heaves and shifts—my boy is sick with affect with bloodstream
    expanses of water

Run from his knife, run from my boy over the soil and pierce his
    thigh
to soak the earth, a body of iron swings from the tree
heaves and shifts—my boy is sick with affect—with bloodstream
    expanses of water
teeming with bodies butchered stript and littered—rendered so

To soak the earth a body of iron. Swings from the tree
my boy enclosed within its fruits—his body teems and shifts
teems with bodies butchered stript and littered—rendered so
bodies becoming other bodies breathe *my boy is sick*

ARS POETICA

Here, in the gully of your youth
O beloved substitute

lies ragged ear and broken tooth
tooth for tooth for pocket knife—

the bright red thresher
that field of grasses

and Love, in my head
lies a great sea

There, where brain engages bone
and green water stills between shores

under the low dome
of brown sky

In your head: The sketched
ship with one waving sail

and *who predicts the future*
by observing a flock of birds?

Still the question: Which of us
will conjur the man, his body

a cream X, his neck a white wingspan
face downturned, bailing

the storm behind him
and the same painted ship

Love, we have flown
to the edge of this ocean

the sky was full of planes
Curled sleeping here, my ear

floods and over my head
above my head, the weeping flock aligns

ENVOI

that we clutched upon   the word, thus adorned, bodies forth
    itself
And posed at a canal; the sea careens, the sea is an ear
hold with your arms yourself, adorn.
And we are driven, we are driven here
past the glens of industry—a ring of colored lights shelters a hill
    each mile or so
a little fire in a wild field
or—a hot pink bra, my rings and glasses
Across the green field spread rows of straight lines as big around as
    my bared wrist
parsing out power to the counties
or—we told jokes to release emotion
The two fields in semantic tableaux: green crop and red earth
    made common by water
or—if X were here, would he...? and so on
Answer with thy uncovered body adorn
a hum shimmers inches above the grass, the grass cuts into our
    shins fine sickleshapes
above our heads, sound from the power lines
if X were here... (*continues*)

TYRANNY OF THE MUSE

And it shows a compass and it shows a clock
and it shows a compass and it shows a clock
and it shows the hour and the hour burning
And it shows a compass and it shows a clock
and it shows a book become the face of a man
and it shows the boy's face *I ran as fast as I could*
and it shows the bird in the boy's heart *I ran*
and I ran is Jacksonville burning
And I ran the white boat
and I ran the length of your arm outstretched of your back
fled your back fled
and I fled the hour and the hour burning
and it shows a compass and it shows a clock
I fled the body the burning room
I fled the bare tree
I fled singing
washing in perfect congress with his body
I fled *Dear Schellmann* conducting a child to school
conducting the boy into the boat I fled
and I fled I pushed I fled
the burnt flesh the seared flesh an illustration outstretched
and it shows a compass and it shows a clock
and it shows a man burning *beloved*
my beloved is me
and it shows the boy at fifty paces
and I fled
and I fled
and I fled

NOTES

Tyranny of Errant Desire: "Take heed, sirrah, the whip" is borrowed from *King Lear*, and is Lear's threat to his Fool.

Misread: the last line is taken from Pound's translation of Li-Po's poem, "The River Merchant's Wife: A Letter."

To the Trees' Irregular Tremor: owes a debt to James Wright's poem "Sitting in a Small Screen House on a Summer Morning."

Tyranny of the Aerial Map: the line "I am a blasted tree" is from Mary Shelley's *Frankenstein*.

Abandoned Paradelle: was inspired, in part, by Paul O. Zelinsky's retelling and illustrations of *Rapunzel*.

Lines Reclaimed from Faith: borrows the phrase "for the birds that see him, for their feasts' delight" from *Antigone*.

Desire: borrows the phrase "always the soft idiot, softly, me" from "Law, Say the Gardeners, Is the Sun," by W. H. Auden.

Invective: owes a debt to both Ovid and Berryman.

Envoi: "a little fire in a wild field" is from *King Lear*.